Mies van der Rohe

Farnsworth House

Residential Masterpieces 30
Mies van der Rohe
Farnsworth House

Text and edited by Yoshio Futagawa
Photographed by Yukio Futagawa
Art direction: Gan Hosoya

Printed and bound in Japan

ISBN 978-4-87140-563-8 C1352

Mies van der Rohe
Farnsworth House
Plano, Illinois, U.S.A., 1945-51

Text by Yoshio Futagawa

Photographed by Yukio Futagawa

世界現代住宅全集30

ミース・ファン・デル・ローエ
ファンズワース邸
アメリカ合衆国，イリノイ州，プラーノ　1945-51

文・編集：二川由夫

企画・撮影：二川幸夫

アメリカに建てられた神殿——二川由夫
A Pantheon in America *by Yoshio Futagawa*

1938年秋，ミースはロッテルダムの港からヨーロッパを後にし，アメリカに向かった。モダニズムの理念，バウハウスでの教鞭，そして多くのユダヤ人クライアントやアーティスト，左翼文化人たちとの交流などによって祖国ドイツを掌握していたナチスから目を付けられていたところ，アメリカからの招聘を受ける形であるものの，ある種の「亡命」をしたのだった。この「亡命」を境に建築家としてのキャリアは大きく二つの時代＝ヨーロッパとアメリカでの活動に分けられることになり，この二つの時代における仕事は明解にコントラストのあるものとなるが，共に戦前／戦後の建築界を牽引し続ける，影響力の強いものとなった。

　1929年のスペイン，バルセロナで催された国際博覧会でのドイツ館であった仮設建築，通称「バルセロナ・パヴィリオン」(1929年)はミースの戦前／ヨーロッパ時代における最高傑作の一つである。床と屋根は抽象化されて純度が上げられ，その間に置かれる壁面は美しいマテリアルのテクスチャーが纏わされ，それらがつくり出した空間構成や質は，新しい建築理論のマニフェストであり，その後の建築界に多大な影響を与え続けるプロトタイプとなった。

　アメリカに移住したミースはシカゴを拠点に勢力的に活動し，SOMをはじめとして多くの「信者」を生み，アメリカのみならず世界中の建築を牽引した。アメリカでの仕事の多くは，ヨーロッパ時代，紙上に構想された数々のプロジェクトを源流とし，それらがアメリカナイズされて実現されたと言える。大量消費の戦勝国ならではの供給豊富な鋼材やガラスを用い，規格材の特性をディテールに反映させ，さらにそれらを美学的に昇華させた建築のプロダクトであった。「ファンズワース邸」(1945-51年)のH型鋼の柱が2枚のスラブを外側で支持する様は，まさにアメリカ時代のミースが手がけた「イリノイ工科大学クラウンホール」(1950-56年)から後年の「ベルリン国立近代美術館」(1968年)までの一連の建物のプロトタイプであり，それ以上の存在——それ自体で輝きを持った建築の神殿であり，その後の未来への予言であり，揺るがない絶対的な普遍性の提示としての戦後最高の傑作建築の一つである。

　1945年，シカゴの著名な女性精神科医，エディス・ファンズワース博士はミースに週末住宅の設計を依頼した。敷地はシカゴ市街から西に90キロほど行ったプラーノの町，手付かずの自然の森であった。敷地は長手北側に沿って幹線道路，南側に沿ってフォックス川が流れている。3.9ヘクタールの敷地にはこの地方によくある大きな木々や，春夏秋を彩る草花が豊富に植生

In the fall of 1938, Mies left Europe from the Port of Rotterdam and headed for the United States. Because of his modernist ideas, his position as the director of Bauhaus, and his interactions with many Jewish clients, artists, and left-wing cultural figures, he was being watched by the Nazis controlling Germany, his homeland. Thus, although Mies's relocation was done in response to an invitation from the United States, it was, in reality, a kind of exile. This de-facto exile divided his career into two major periods: the European and the American. A clear contrast exists between Mies's works from the two periods, but both groups of works were highly influential, and they led the architectural world both before and after the war.

The German pavilion temporarily built for the World's Fair hosted in Barcelona, Spain, in 1929, commonly known as *the Barcelona Pavilion*, is one of Mies's pre-war masterpieces designed during his time in Europe. The floor and roof were abstracted and refined, and the walls dividing the space between them were adorned with textures of beautiful materials. The spatial composition and quality they created proposed a new architectural theory, and they became a prototype that continues to enormously influence the architectural world.

After emigrating to the United States, Mies based himself in Chicago and worked as an architect. He attracted many followers, including SOM, and led the American and global architectural world. Most of his works in the United States were Americanized versions of the projects he had conceived of during his time in Europe. For these architectural products, Mies used steel and glass, which were abundantly available in the United States, the victorious country of mass consumption. He incorporated the characteristics of these standardized materials into details and then aesthetically sublimated them. How the H-beams of *the Farnsworth House* (1945-51) support the two slabs from the outside is prototypical; the same style can be found in a series of buildings Mies designed during his American era, from *the Crown Hall of the Illinois Institute of Technology* (1950-56) to *the New National Gallery in Berlin* (1968). *The Farnsworth House* is in reality something more than a prototype—it is a pantheon of architecture that shines on its own, a revelation of the future that will follow, and one of the greatest masterpieces of post-war architecture demonstrating an unwavering, absolute universality.

In 1945, Dr. Edith Farnsworth, a prominent psychiatrist in Chicago, commissioned Mies to design a weekend home. The site was in an untouched forest in the town of Plano, about 90 kilometers west of downtown Chicago. There is a highway running along the north side of the site and the Fox River on the

し，冬に落葉し，時に雪に埋もれ，荒涼とした風景を見せる。喧騒の大都会，シカゴを逃れ，週末を過ごすのには最高の贅沢な場所であった。そこで，クライアントは近代建築の記念碑的な建物を建てたいと望み，ニューヨークの近代美術館に相談したところ，三人の巨匠，コルビュジエ，ライト，そしてミースを紹介された。クライアントはシカゴに居たミースに依頼する。建築家の創造の自由を尊重すべく，機能については最小限の要求がなされた。週末住宅の初期案は翌46年にはでき上がったものの工事はすぐには行われず，49年9月に起工，51年に完成している。

　週末住宅は一対の長方形スラブがずらされた形で東西軸，つまりフォックス川の流れに沿うように配置されている。南側のすぐ脇にはシュガーメイプルの大木が立ち，これらの木々が落とす大きな影は夏場，住宅内部の快適性に少なからず貢献したが，2013年失われた。南側のテラスとなるスラブは間口55フィート（16.76メートル），奥行き22フィート（6.71メートル）である。北側，同じ大きさの屋根が上部に架けられたスラブは，間口77フィート（23.47メートル），奥行き29フィート（8.84メートル），その上に四方をガラス壁に囲われた居室部分と半屋外空間であるポーチが配置される。ポーチと居住部分は長手

面の両側に4本ずつH型鋼の柱が22フィート（6.71メートル）間隔で建てられ，天井高は9フィート6インチ（2.90メートル）。フォックス川は氾濫して敷地が浸水することがわかっていたため，週末住宅の居室の床面は地表レベルより5フィート3インチ（1.60メートル），テラスはそれより低い2フィート11インチ（0.89メートル）持ち上げられることになった（それでも床上浸水の洪水は幾たびか起こっている）。それぞれのスラブと地表は階段で結ばれる。それぞれのスラブは2フィート×2フィート6インチ（61センチ×76センチ）のトラバーチンが貼られ，石板の目地がつくるグリッドに沿って各部の寸法は決定された。床／屋根スラブを構成する鉄骨の四周を回っているガーターの見付は同じ，1フィート3インチ（38センチ）である。居住部を囲う板ガラスはガーター面に沿って配置され，その厚みは1/4インチ（6.35ミリ），幅は10フィート6インチ（3.20メートル）の大きさを持つ。

　施工は例外的な高精度が要求され，躯体は現場溶接されたのち，その表面をサンドブラストによって磨かれた後，白色に塗装され，工業規格材であるH型鋼は抽象化された。

　週末住宅へのアプローチは，敷地北側の道路から木々や緑の豊富なラン

south side. The 3.9-ha site had huge trees native to the region; flowers that blossomed in the spring, summer, and autumn; and trees that shed their leaves in the winter and sometimes became buried in the snow, causing a desolate landscape to appear. Offering a perfect escape from the hustle and bustle of Chicago, the enchanting place was an incomparable sanctuary to spend the weekend in. The client's intention was to build something that was akin to a monument to modern architecture. When she consulted with the Museum of Modern Art in New York, she was introduced to three master architects: Le Corbusier, Wright, and Mies. Dr. Farnsworth chose Mies, who was in Chicago. She kept functional requirements to a bare minimum to respect the architect's creative freedom. Although the initial plan for the weekend house was completed in 1946, construction did not begin immediately, and it instead started in September 1949. The house was completed in 1951.

The weekend house consists of a pair of off-set rectangular slabs arranged along the east-west axis along the Fox River. Tall sugar maple trees stood by the south side, and although one of them was lost in 2013, while they existed, the large shadows cast by them helped provide a comfortable environment inside the house. The terrace on the south side has a width of 55 feet (16.76 meters) and a length of 22 feet (6.71

meters). On the north side, a slab with a roof of the same size has a frontage of 77 feet (23.47 meters) and a length of 29 feet (8.84 meters). On top of it is the living area surrounded on four sides by glass walls and a semi-outdoor porch. Along the porch and the living area are the H-steel columns, four in intervals of 22 feet (6.71 meters) on both of the longitudinal sides. The ceiling height is 9′6″ (2.90 meters). The site adjacent to the Fox River was known to flood, so the weekend house was designed with a floor raised 5′3″ (1.60 meters) above the ground and a terrace 2′11″ (0.89 meters) lower than the floor level. (The house has nevertheless become flooded on several occasions.) The slabs and the ground surface are connected by stairs. Each slab was tiled with travertine 2′ x 2′6″ (61 cm x 76 cm) and the dimensions of other elements were determined along the grid created by the masonry joints. The dimension of the structural steel girders enveloping the four sides of the floor and roof slabs is 1′3″ (38 cm). The plate-glass surrounding the living area is installed along the girders and is 1/4″ (6.35 mm) thick and 10′6″ (3.20 meters) wide.

The construction of the weekend house required exceptionally high precision. The structural skeleton was welded on-site, then the surface was sandblasted and painted white to abstract the H-beams, a standardized industrial material.

ドスケープに進み入り，建物の南側に回り込むように進んで行く。テラスと
ポーチに架けられた一対の階段を南から北へ，一直線に登ると，中央より南
側に1フィート（30.48センチ）寄せられた両開きのガラスの玄関ドアを右手に見
ることになる。

　住宅は基本的に四方をガラス壁に囲われた水槽のような一室空間で，中
央より北西に寄った所に配置された，プリマヴェーラというオーク材の一種
で仕上げられたコアによって，空間は食堂，居間，寝室，台所のエリアに緩
やかに分けられている。コアは二つの浴室を東西の内部に，北側面に台所
が組み込まれ，南側中央には居間のための暖炉が配置され，内部中央には
床暖房用のボイラーが隠されている。コアの高さは天井面より低く抑えられ
て，独立したヴォリュームのように扱われている（暖炉とボイラーの煙突のために
その中央では天井面と繋がっている。これらの煙突は外部においてその高さは抑えら
れ，建物外部の周囲から見ることはできない）。居間の東側にはクライアントの希望
に応え，もう一つの低いキャビネットが置かれ，その背後は書斎として使わ
れていた（後年このキャビネットは90度向きが変えられて，寝室のプライヴァシー保護の
ための目隠しとして使われた）。

2020年に行われたインスタレーションで，ファンズワース博士がどのような
設えでこの週末住宅を使っていたかが再現されていた様子を見ると，ミース
が仕立て上げた完璧なプロポーションの絶対的空間がまったく異質のテイス
トの家具群に満たされていたことが窺える。ミースと博士との関係は依頼当
時から数年の間の親密な距離（恋愛関係にあったとも言われている）から，竣工後
には訴訟へと至るほど悪化し，ある種，憎悪を持って施主はこの家で過ご
したことが想像される。関係の悪化と共に，この住宅の性能面での問
題——冬期の床暖房の性能不足，夏期の換気不足や遮れない陽光などに対
処するべく，ポーチには川からの蚊の大群の侵入を防ぐ網戸が付けられ，
カーテンで四方のガラス面は閉ざされて使われることになった。

　博士の憎悪とは裏腹にこの週末住宅は建築界では絶賛され，多くの建築
関係者がひと目見ようとフォックス川の対岸を訪れたことは想像に難くない。
1972年，ロンドンのデヴェロッパー，ピーター・パランボ氏がこの家を購入し
た。パランボ氏はコルビュジエ，ライトの住宅も所有した言わば建築のパト
ロンである。ミースにも最大級の敬意を持っていた新しい家主は，愛憎劇
の後をクリアランスした。網戸を外し，周囲のランドスケープも整備し，初め

The weekend house's approach begins at the road on the north of the site. It enters a lush landscape of trees and greenery and then curves to reach the south side of the building. If one walks from south to north straight up the stairs on the terrace and porch, one will see to the right a glazed double-door entrance located 1 foot (30.48 cm) to the south from the center.

The house is basically an aquarium-like single room enveloped by glass walls on all sides, loosely divided into areas for dining, living, sleeping, and cooking by a core finished with an oak material called Primavera located to the northwest of the center. The core features two bathrooms to the east and west, a kitchen to the north, a fireplace for the living room to the center of the south side, and a boiler for radiant floor heating hidden in the center. The height of the core is kept lower than the ceiling surface and is treated as an independent volume (It is connected to the ceiling in the center to serve as the chimneys for the fireplace and boiler. The exterior height of these chimneys is kept short so that they cannot be seen by a person standing near the building). As per the client's request, a low cabinet was added to the east side of the living room, and the space behind it was used as a study (This cabinet was later turned around 90 degrees and used as a screen to provide privacy to the occupants of the bedroom).

In 2020, how Dr. Farnsworth used this weekend house was revealed through an installation. The absolute space with perfect proportions Mies created was filled with furniture of a completely different aesthetic. The intimate relationship between Mies and the doctor (some claim it was a romantic relationship) lasted for several years from the time of Mies's commission. The relationship then soured, and both parties ultimately sued each other after the completion of the house. It is not difficult to imagine that the client lived in the house, harboring terrible resentment. As the relationship between Mies and the doctor deteriorated, the functional issues of this house, such as insufficient floor heating in winter, inadequate ventilation in summer, and unlockable sunlight, became evident. A screen door was installed to prevent mosquitoes from coming in from the river, and the curtains were kept shut behind the glass walls.

Contrary to the doctor's extreme bitterness, the weekend house was applauded by the architectural world, and many visitors arrived on the other side of the Fox River to get a glimpse of the house. In 1972, Peter Palumbo, a developer from London, bought the weekend house. A patron of architecture who also owns houses by Le Corbusier and Wright, Lord Palumbo, who had the greatest respect for Mies, erased the marks the love-

てこの家にミースがデザインした家具群を入れて，巨匠がこの家で描いた理想の世界がここに実現／完成された（パランボ氏は2003年にこの週末住宅をナショナル・トラストに売却した）。

　洪水対策というプラクティカルな理由に加えて，持ち上げられたテラスや居室部分の床レベルは周囲の自然環境との良好な関係性に大きく寄与している。高低差がつけられた2枚のトラバーチンのスラブはアイレベルと地上高を十分に考慮され，空中に浮かぶかのような絶妙な位置に浮かび，周囲のランドスケープや通り抜ける風は遮られることなく建物の下を通り抜けている。周囲の自然との間に，絶妙の「間合い」が生まれると同時に建築と自然のコンテクストとの融合と拡張解釈が生まれているという両義性は，解像度の低い，写真やヴィデオなどのイメージやテキストでは到底表現できるものではない。ある種の神秘性，神々しい存在に昇華されているのだ。そしてプロトタイプとしての週末住宅は多義的な解釈と無限に拡張されるような可能性を秘めたものとして，多くの議論を生み，フォロワーたちの創造の手掛かりにされ，様々なバリエーションがつくられた。18世紀ヨーロッパの古典リバイバリズムのパヴィリオンの基壇に見立てられ，また，高床が日本の伝統

建築の地表／環境との距離感を彷彿させると論じられた。そして，アメリカの「ケース・スタディ・ハウス」（1945–66年）をはじめ，多くの鉄骨造建築，そして住宅建築のマニュアルとなった。

　「バルセロナ・パヴィリオン」がヨーロッパ建築の歴史的背景，分脈を踏まえて発信された艶やかな深みを持ったマニフェストとすれば，「ファンズワース邸」は，アメリカの新文化が戦後，世界的な標準になっていく状況により即して，強い明快さを持って発信されたマニフェストであった。ミースはアメリカ「亡命」によって母国語であるドイツ語を奪われ，さほど上手くない英語で建築を説明するとき，それは拡大解釈されて深遠で哲学的に響き，神格化されていったこと，そのことは自覚していただろう。

　Less is More。「ファンズワース邸」はグローバルに響く建築の神殿となった。

hate drama left behind. The screen doors were removed, the surrounding landscape was improved, and the furniture designed by Mies was placed in the house for the first time to finally realize and complete the ideal world dreamed of by the house's creator (Palumbo sold the weekend house to the National Trust for Historic Preservation in 2003).

In addition to being a practical anti-flood feature, the elevated terrace and the floor level of the interior living area significantly contribute to the beautiful harmony that exists between the weekend house and the surrounding natural environment. When defining the two travertine slabs with different heights, the eye level and ground clearance were thoroughly considered so that the slabs will hover in midair in a perfect position as if they were floating in the air. The surrounding landscape and the wind pass under the building without being obstructed. An exquisite recess is created between the building and the surrounding nature; simultaneously, a fusion and an extended interpretation of the building and nature and their contexts appear. Such ambiguity cannot be expressed using low-resolution images and texts, such as photographs and videos. The site has been exalted into a kind of mysterious and divine being. The weekend house is recognized as a prototype with infinite interpretations and possibilities. It has aroused

much controversy, become a source of creative inspiration for followers, and has had diverse variations of it made. It was also likened to the pavilion of classical revivalism in 18th century Europe, and some argued the raised floor was reminiscent of the distance between the surface and the environment found in traditional Japanese architecture. Finally, it became a "manual" for many steel-structured buildings and residential buildings, including *the Case Study Houses* (1945-66) in the United States.

If *the Barcelona Pavilion* was a manifesto with a lustrous depth that was based on the historical background and context of European architecture, *the Farnsworth House* was a strong and straight-forward manifesto that took into consideration the post-war situation of the new American culture that was becoming the global standard. Mies was made to explain Architecture in his not-so-fluent English, as his de-facto exile to America took his native German language away from him. As he explained, he was probably aware that the listeners were overthinking his words, that his speech probably sounded profound and philosophical to them, and he was becoming a god to them.

Less is More. *The Farnsworth House* became a pantheon of architecture, and its influence resonated the world over.

English translation by Haruki Makio

View toward Farnsworth House over Fox River, April 2009

Banks of Fox River which floods frequently, April 2009

View from approach, early 1970s

View toward entrance in fall, early 1970s

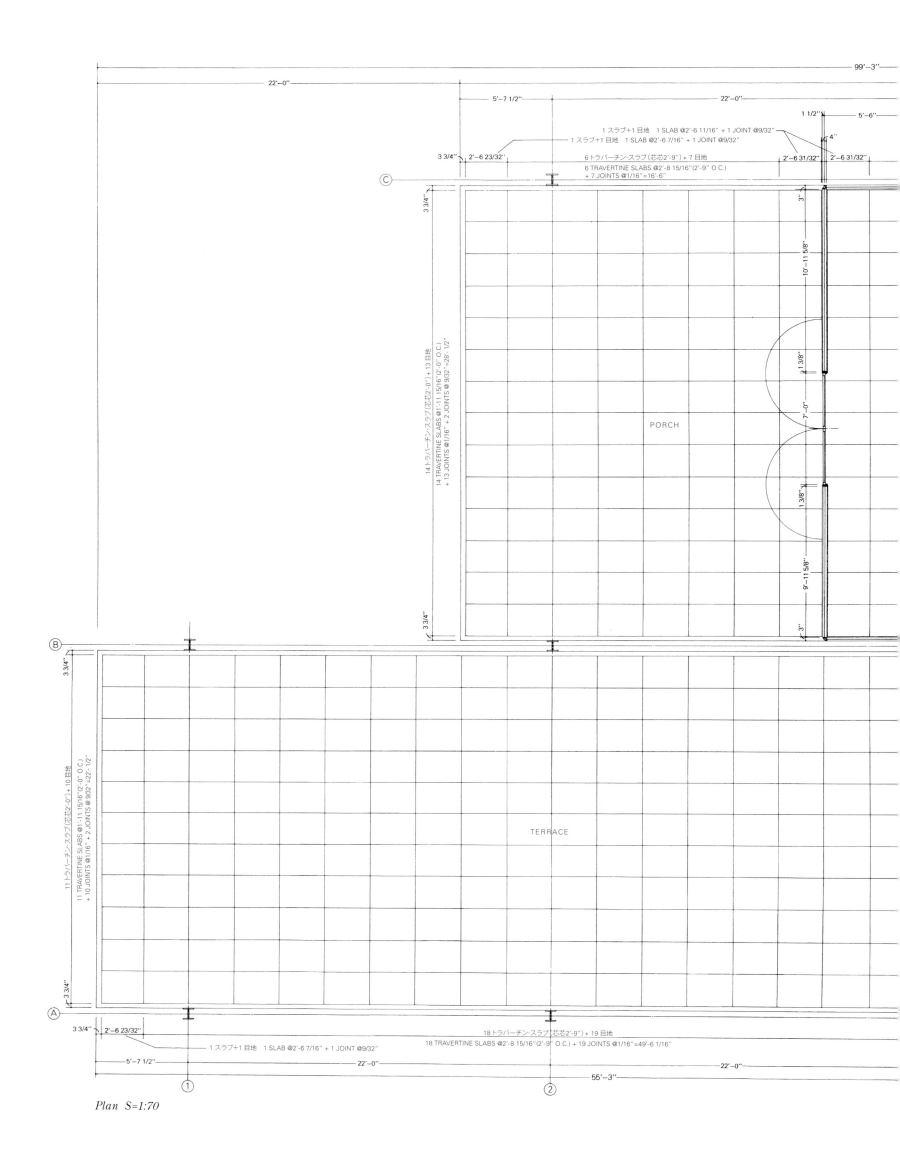

Plan S=1:70

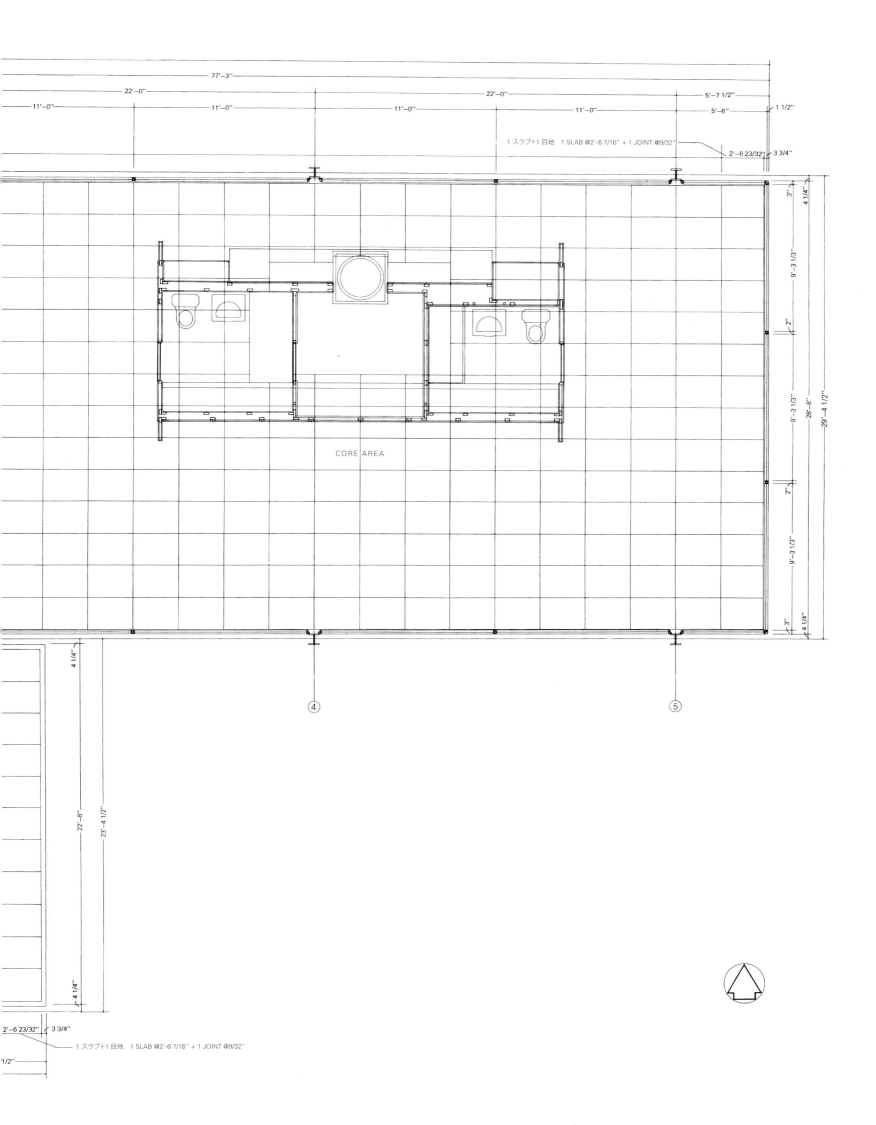

CORE AREA

1 スラブ+1 目地 1 SLAB @2'-6 7/16" + 1 JOINT @9/32"

77'–3"

22'–0"
22'–0"
5'–7 1/2"

11'–0"
11'–0"
11'–0"
11'–0"
5'–6"
1 1/2"

2'–6 23/32" 3 3/4"

3"
4 1/4"

9'–3 1/3"

2"

9'–3 1/3"

28'–8"
29'–4 1/2"

2"

9'–3 1/3"

3"
4 1/4"

④
⑤

4 1/4"

22'–8"
23'–4 1/2"

4 1/4"

2'–6 23/32" 3 3/4"

1 スラブ+1 目地 1 SLAB @2'-6 7/16" + 1 JOINT @9/32"

1/2"

View toward entrance in winter, January 1997

Terrace inbetween ground and main house, early 1970s

Raised main volume. Terrace and steps to porch, early 1970s

Terrace, early 1970s

Underfloor with height of 4 feet (1.219 meter), June 2001

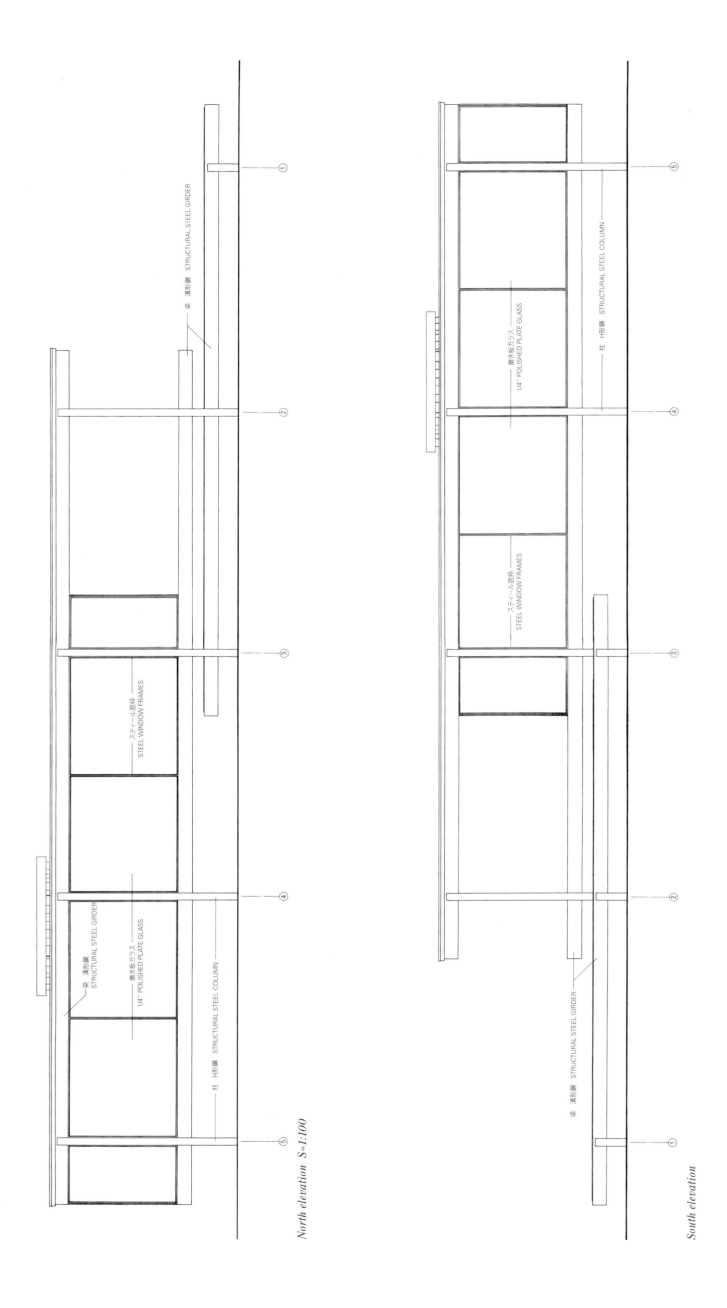

梁 溝形鋼 STRUCTURAL STEEL GIRDER

スティール窓枠 STEEL WINDOW FRAMES

梁 溝形鋼 STRUCTURAL STEEL GIRDER
磨き板ガラス 1/4" POLISHED PLATE GLASS

柱 H形鋼 STRUCTURAL STEEL COLUMN

North elevation *S=1:100*

磨き板ガラス 1/4" POLISHED PLATE GLASS

スティール窓枠 STEEL WINDOW FRAMES

柱 H形鋼 STRUCTURAL STEEL COLUMN

梁 溝形鋼 STRUCTURAL STEEL GIRDER

South elevation

Porch and H steel column, early 1970s

Porch and entrance, early 1970s

Porch. Looking north, early 1970s

Entrance, June 2001

Looking through interior from porch, April 2009

View toward porch, early 1970s

Dining room, early 1970s

View toward Fox River from dining room, April 2009

Living room, June 2001

Living room, early 1970s

Cabinet houses core. Fireplace on center, April 2009

H structural steel column, April 2009

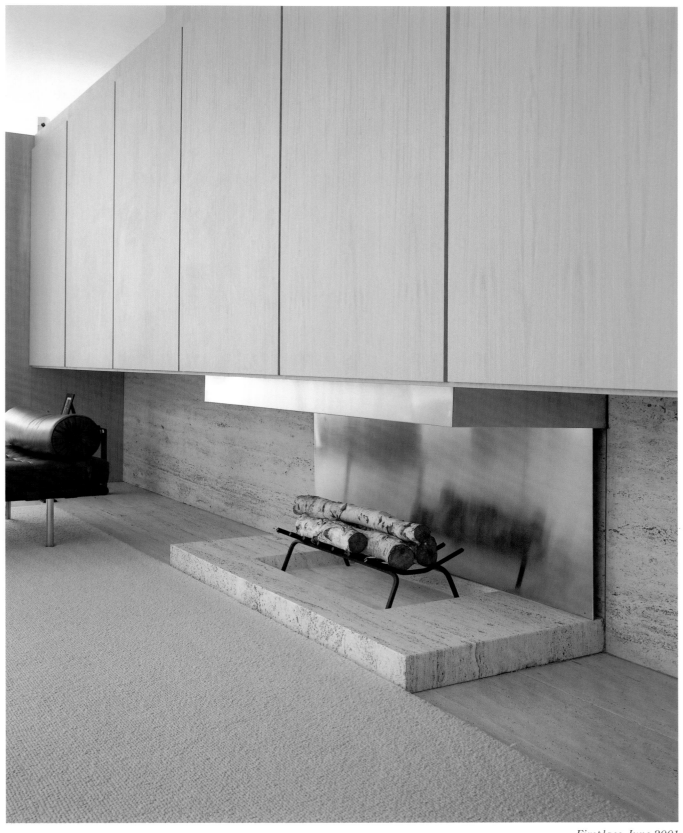

Fireplace, June 2001

Looking through dining room and kitchen from porch, April 2009

Kitchen, early 1970s

Corner of bedroom. Living room on right, early 1970s

Bathroom, early 1970s

Windows of bedroom, June 2001

Bedroom, early 1970s

Partial north elevation. View toward bedroom and kitchen, early 1970s

North elevation, April 2009

View toward porch. Dining room on left, October 1994

Overall view from northwest, early 1970s

Fox River, View from property of Farnsworth House, June 2001

世界現代住宅全集 30
ミース・ファン・デル・ローエ
ファンズワース邸
2020 年 10 月 23 日発行
文・編集：二川由夫
撮影：二川幸夫
アート・ディレクション：細谷巖

印刷・製本：大日本印刷株式会社
制作・発行：エーディーエー・エディタ・トーキョー
151-0051　東京都渋谷区千駄ヶ谷 3-12-14
TEL. (03) 3403-1581 (代)

禁無断転載

ISBN 978-4-87140-563-8 C1352